SEVASTOPOL:

On Photographs of War

poems by

William Allen

XENOS BOOKS

For information:
Xenos Books
P.O. Box 52152
Riverside, California 92517-3152

Library of Congress Cataloging-in-Publication Data
Allen, William, 1957-
   Sevastopol : on photographs of war / William Allen.
      p. cm.
   Photographs (taken 1847-1997) on one page with commentary by
   the author on the opposite page.
   ISBN 1-879378-30-2. -- ISBN 1-879378-29-9 (pbk.)
   1. War poetry, American. 2. War--Pictorial works. I. Title.
   PS3551.L438S48 1997
   811'.54--dc21   97-20264
                                            CIP

Cover: detail from Dmitri Baltermans, Citizens Exchange Council
Cover and book design by the author

Printed by Thomson-Shore,
Dexter, Michigan 48130-9701
Set in Adobe Garamond

ALSO BY WILLIAM ALLEN
The Man on the Moon, Poems,
New York University and Persea Press, 1987

This book was funded in part with the generous support
of the Sonia Raiziss-Giop Foundation

Thanks, for sustenance, especially to my family,
howsoever they appear in this book, to Elizabeth and Lotti Allen,
Michael Dinwiddie, Mike Glier, Patricia Spears Jones, Alfredo
de Palchi, Jan Freeman, Marjory Wentworth,
Barbara Westermann—and Philip Levine.

And thanks to the following publications for permission to reprint:

Chelsea—"Grief, Kerch," "Fight to the Death," "Burial at Sea,"
"Sowjetunion," and "Photographer Photographing a Dead Horse"
Poetry East—"Heartbreak Hotel," "Bones, Joints, Flat Feet,"
and "Heartbreak Hotel"
New Observations—"Joe Louis in Italy, 1944"

Table of Contents

I

II

III

About the Author

for Virginia Fairfield Warren Allen—
(1902-1997) artist, architect
of souls, beloved wife

I

We work in the dark—we do what we can—we give what we have.

Henry James, "The Middle Years"

Photographer Unknown, Amon Carter Museum

PLACE IN THE SUN OF THE SON OF HENRY CLAY

This burnt plate is place in the sun of the son of Henry Clay,
a spit-earth burial in Monterrey, in the mesquite of Hidalgo
up at Encantada, where bones of the whoreson Rebs
are sucked by robbers plucking teeth and amulets
off the dead of Los Lobos, mourned by angels Whittier
called *souls of the emphatic,* slave trade gone
to grapeshot wounds for another American monsoon.
Zach Taylor's made Homeric here, as dog-trot rhythms
of Trafalgar bear this son of anti-abolitionists home.
Before the Great Revival, a brother's breakdown
at Blue Licks Spa brings ague to the senator, his pistols
packed are signature the boy's body travels by North
to Nachitoches, back to the family plot at Ashland,
out by the conical ice-house where he as a boy
chased thoroughbreds. That bit of whooping cough
at West Point did him in in Santa Ana's noose
of captive infantry: coffee-slack, green-scurvied pool
of pickled pork, a sutler's blood in embers
by the cookfire, last affaire d'coeur before the dust
of ritual embalm. Son of Clay or Apollo or Abraham,
rest in peace now, in the arms of an absent howling mother.

Roger Fenton, Library of Congress

IN THE VALLEY OF THE SHADOW OF DEATH

Ezekiel's bones, dried to dust beyond this cusp of hill
where a pock-mouthed dawn wakes all Sevastopol,
and every hillock hides a thousand faces of the sky,
where young men's corpses stink, and American nurses
sweat to make love to Sardinian boys on horses
from Balaclava, by Russian cannon shot that missed
its mark. Here, the treeless landscape looms
along a precipice of fear, this first doomed
project of the photograph, a tongue
of the Ottoman Empire waggling out salt
from the Black Sea: Crimea, 1854, home
of the last-tamed pig of the fireweed earth,
a theater for war, a black crude, blue cornfield,
where the Danube *U's* and slickens, falls
to the plundering Balkan bears,
where buzzards pick at sinews of the last
three hundred of the Light Brigade,
in a valley that hides from the moon.
Then from below comes the sound of scorpions,
the prairie hens who cock their heads and wait
for the sun to rise upon another century.

Mathew Brady, Library of Congress

DUNKER CHURCH, ANTIETAM

For Melville, on Malvern Hill the elms would speak
tetrameter to orient the infamy that day. For others,
brothers tromping stone-arc aqueducts to Fredericksburg,
the eye of the soul is still on ice. Here, near Samuel
Mumma's farm, the white-brick Dunker Church
is an Anabaptist seat of fire, off one lumbering
Sunken Road, taking hits from both sides—this is
a hospice for amputees and aftermath. Each convert
gets baptised three times, each reader dunked
in verse, image, music of the antebellum troposphere:
father, son, no Holy Ghost. The limber chest
is empty, artillery spent on the 23,000 who died
in a border slave state's Pyrrhic song. Besides
McClelland's blister sores and Lee's wandering eye,
there's nothing left but clarion call, bent over
a dozen dooryards where incantation blooms,
infesting the shoeless Confederate dead, painting
a mirror image of this picture: song of the self
one slave song past the height of the elms,
as they rain down leaf and seed upon what's
greening in this page of sediments and sorrow.

Eadweard Muybridge, National Archives

TULE LAKE LAVA BEDS, THE MODOC WARS

Time is motion, energy, stress, and speed, divided by the sun's
circumference at half past equinox tonight: so say
the Muybridge sequenced photographs of pregnant maids
who elbow dumbweights, or knock-kneed men stepping
up footstools in a watercolor squat. Before these
ambrotypes, the artist set his tripods up in lava beds
for the army, in a dry-bone valley of bell tents
blowing against a Cenozoic drainage of salt-flat seas.
For months, a band of Indian outsiders with breech-
fed rifles sucked rye grass, burning down manifest destiny
along the borders of now and the nineteenth century.
Later the heads of Captain Jack and Boston Charley
are shipped to a medical museum back East.
Here Muybridge plants an enemy Klamath scout in
an igneous gash of rock, to simulate a battle, the yield
and amplitude of war—never yet caught
with a candid eye. And others rebels, Barncho and Sloluck,
are box-carred off to Alcatraz, as the Modoc myths
of stealing fire—Lost River Blind Man's bet
with one-eyed Watchman—are spent in Coehorn mortar,
and the desert music wavers, unmetered and unspoke.

John Grabill, Library of Congress

BRULE VILLAGE, WOUNDED KNEE

This is no forest primeval: Badlands, Black Hills, a month
beyond the Pine Ridge tragedy. Arroyo clefts, a moon
popping trees. Shush now. Spring is on the way. In rivulets,
just cold pastoral, a fog's memory of 1890. Shoshoni ponies
in sheep sorrel, shacklebone wrists up-twisted, black ice
after bloody mud and blizzard, the two-dollar cleanup later.
Remington was there for Harper's, along with Gatling guns,
relic hunters, government draymen, to document this last
resistance to the dog-faced whites. Was it shittimwood,
a Christ in a bullet-proof ghost dance weasel shirt, voices
of the eld Wovoka up from mid-Nevada? Beef issue day:
gut-whet curlicues of smoke from Mousseau's kitchen
chimney. In the bed of the lead wagon, Big Foot
spits up to the bickering of the Minneconjou Sioux.
Blanket of white atuft the buffalo tundra:
soon it's 1973 and the FBI takes aim
at AIM and fires again. WORLD FAMOUS INDIAN VILLAGE—
shacks and too much corn gin. The aftermath of both
is what's seen in this serene scene at Porcupine Creek.
An Episcopal church still hospital? Scrofula is caused by gophers.
Beyond the breastworks of the cavalry, resistance of the ice is shale.

Photographer Unknown, courtesy of the author

THREE PIKE STREET

End of century, February thaw, horse stalls of a Delancey cul-de-sac
on Sunday afternoon. This subfloor crawlspace leads straight
to salt-flat estuaries of Brighton Beach, to the world
my littlest brother, who lives for haggis and blood-pudding,
shares with me. We shovel potash and horse shit days,
stocking root cellars moonlit nights: green onions, fat cabbage,
bean sprouts, springes and woodcocks. Suddenly there's
wind-up clocks in every Scots-Irish home but ours.
We pay out sod with lime and nickel: below an opium den,
a porker named Rose is our burnished gold. She snuffles lemon rind
and devilled eggs, nests in the lath and cotton batting
below a brand-new Bilco door. She grubs for sand ants,
half a head of broccoli, tubers and tulip roots,
an honorary member of our race—one that proscribes
the ascent of man. Take note of a cheap-pearled parasol
left by a landlord, and the metastisizing wad of fucking rat.
Here my mind's at home, below a frozen terracotta patio,
below the quare gunk surface of a dream, the politics of greed,
as vegetarians march up Orchard Street, with a giant gherkin
in a spokey pram. The sham's that anything at all has changed:
Rose grunts and pees in sawdust, turns to her curds and whey.

Photographer Unknown, Queens Historical Society

ON NORTH BROTHER ISLAND, HALF-CRAZED
SURVIVORS OF THE WRECK

Beaux-art bas-relief in Tompkins Park commemorates the burning
of the General Slocum; I squint to squirrel out dates—MCMIV—
a year there isn't any war, anywhere on Earth. But this is Panama
at home: the enemy is negligence. East River, workers' Sunday
fête of women and children from St. Mark's Church, the boat
hove to near Hell Gate and spontaneously alit, like tippet tulle
on fire when sun refracts off broken glass. In my dream
the steamer always sloughs up past Rikers before imploding
into ash—baskets of roulade, kegs of stout, ten Kasseler hams
unfeathering in flames across the bowsprit into midships,
babies plunging in life vests into the still-cold churnings
of the river, sinking like stones to the bottom
of the plunge. From the photo you can't hear screams
from in or outside the scarlet fever hospitals, nor along
Longfellow Ave., across the isthmus one boy swims to
to take the brand-new IRT down south to spread news:
rickets, polio, jaundice—now this. All of Little Germany
in black. The sobs from the few surviving mothers
will keep me up another seven centuries, till ghosts
of the wreck merge upwards out of the kill and hover
here, then rise, to where they can try to find some peace.

Photographer Unknown, courtesy of Francis Fralin

PHOTOGRAPHER PHOTOGRAPHING A DEAD HORSE

I do not share your faith in the moral power of exacting
tribute from the war, but this is not the time nor place
for that. This is my gift to you, a postcard taken by
a German amateur, in 1915, in a ghosted village
near Marseilles. It shows an army dilettante,
exposing a film roll of a rotten horse, killed
by the strike of shell fire, ribs poked out
like the hull of a ship or a cheekbone
of the man who preserves this scene.
The well's run dry, the bantams peck
at oystershell, and a lame girl sings.
A grizzled private's shoes shine, another
pouts and scratches at pox on his knees.
But why does the soldier bother a shot
of a socketless bag of bones? Look
and you'll see, unseen, a second old nag,
blown up onto a roof behind them, so placed
to show our amateur the folly of a nature morte,
in trying to image the horrible truth.
So alas, he tries to rescue his brain
through irony, by pushing the camera's button.

Photographer Unknown, Imperial War Museum

IMPRESSION MADE IN THE EARTH AT BILLERICAY, BY COMMANDER WHO FALLS FROM FIERY ZEPPELIN

Like Susan Rothenberg's horses, the image
of the thing becomes the thing itself.
Like patterns of plaid, etched into an arm along
the Nagasaki River, the echo forms
a pool as deep as flood tide surging
through a bevel on the sea. Here,
the lime-parched heather has been hell
and haven to worker ants that tramp
and trellis mountainsides beside the Somme,
where sourgrass flattens and dies
in the imprint of a soldier, true to his vows
of one last cigarette, as enemy flares
streak the night sky. The weight
of his body, pressed into sod, seems almost
Paleozoic by contrast with our own,
when we're flung straight out into air.
Like a child who lies in newly-fallen
snow, he stretches his arms now, salutes
and kicks his heels, wands with his spindly
limbs the wings that take him farther,
farther than we ever want to go.

Photographer Unknown, National Archives

JULY TROUBLES IN PETROGRAD

Like an oscillating wave that gathers its roll
from the sea of Minsk, the crowd pushes its
weight away from itself, drops stragglers
into the outskirts of the pull, skins noses,
shatters iron lampposts, rim-cracked
cisterns of the new-paved boulevards
of Petrograd. The sailors of Kronstadt
bottle-burn the Tauride Palace
where gout-necked socialists swallow
Kerensky's bilgewater, Kronilov's
attempted coups and plots to surrender
Lenin. But farther down the street
where breadlines swell and cobblers
bury the bludgeons of the Black Hundreds
of Lvov, Trotsky sings to Lunacharsky,
to the gathered rubble of women who work
to save the city, this cold summer night
when the moon pulls away from clouds
and the sky wipes clean, and a tide
foams thick with sea-wrack, out of
which the thousands plot their coming.

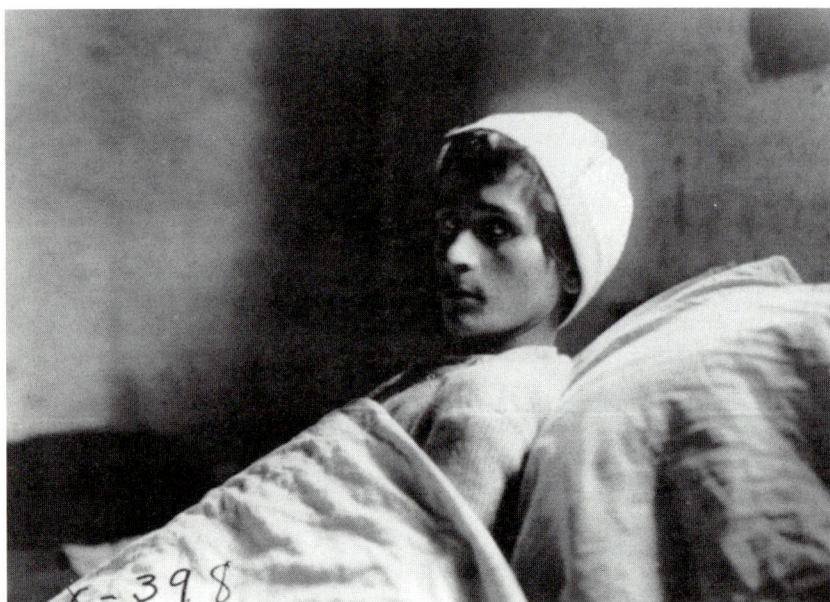

Lewis Hine, Library of Congress

PORTRAIT OF AN ITALIAN SOLDIER

for Harry Nadler (1930-1990)

Giuseppe Ugesi, prisoner at Milowitz
in Austria, is up to his chin in linen sheets,
strapped upright on a hospital cot, with his head
swaddled in gauze to cushion
a swollen cauliflower ear.
Bristles from sunken black sutures
pock his broken aquiline nose,
only a stub remains where his best arm was—
the ghost of which keeps twitching
a finger at a veering cranefly.
He coughs, relieves a cheekful of sputum,
rasps in a gravelly voice for water.
The dark hollows of his eyes flash out
an image of where three roads meet
near Timisoara, where an ambulance caught fire,
the march through droning of cicadas, to here
where his lungs will fill with serum
and collapse, a dam burst that will bring him
to a deeper sleep than counting sheep.
At last, he parts his lips to form a kiss
for all of us who wait for him to speak.

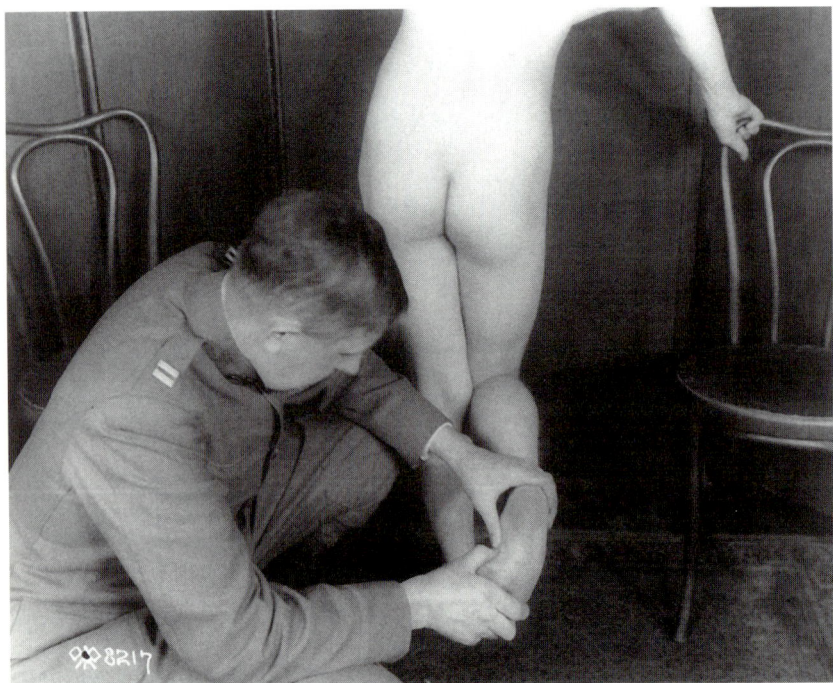

Lt. Reid, U.S. Signal Corps, National Archives

BONES, JOINTS, FLAT FEET

This conscript holds the back of a terrace chair,
standing trouserless and cold, in a damp
examination room at Mercy Hospital.
The intern grips a foot and probes for lumps
or lesions, as if there was a thorn inside,
twisting the knee from its socket joint.
He's fully dressed in uniform for flight,
and cannot see the beauty of this body,
or else he does and does not care,
to send another one off to die. But
the subject of my study is the derriere,
a tight round fist of aubergine,
the hips throned out and restless,
the flesh more supple and pink.
You'd think they'd let him off,
just for this, a prize in any battle
for the sacrament of love. But
the doctor merely scrapes a fingernail
across the ankle and the arch,
finds nothing to prevent the boy
from going, to fly his Kamikaze to the sea.

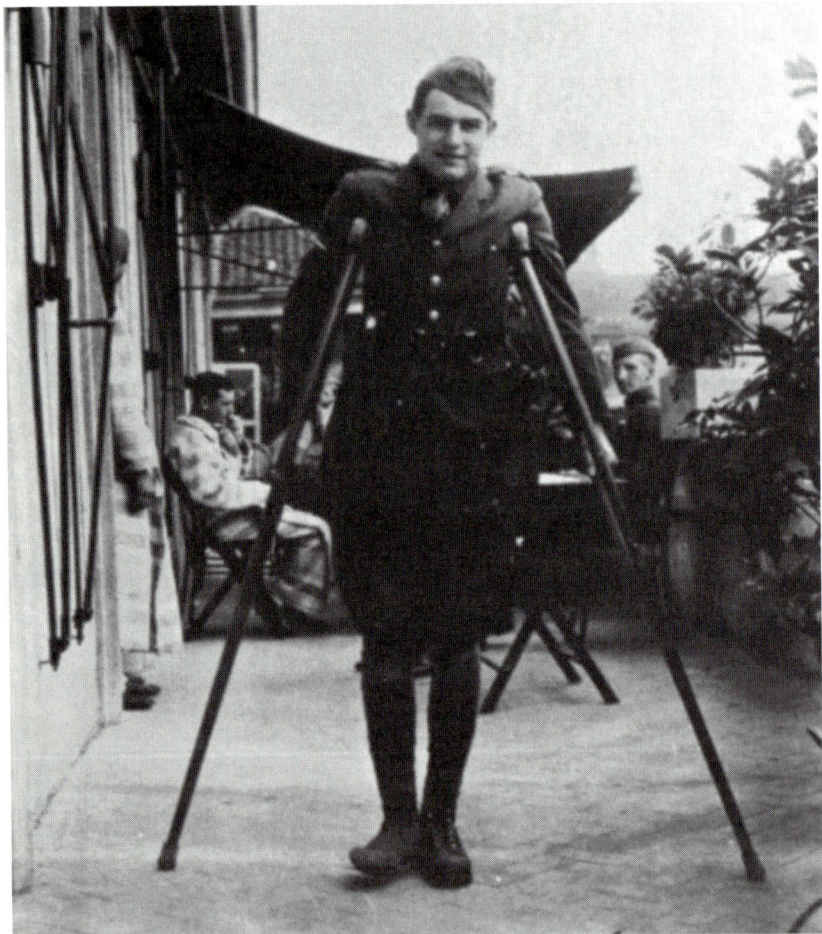

Photographer Unknown, Library of Congress

RIPRENDE LA VITA

for E.E. Allen (1900-1996)

For all the world, this was a man indifferent to all I do,
whose knees at ninety-six still wave about my face,
as he sits in a reclining posture-pedic on a patio,
in thrall to mockingbird in a gecko-
heaven at Riviera Beach. Is it a father's arrogance
or love, the stammering lack of urge to speak:
ministers, slave traders, rum-runners hiding
in mothers' skirts all mute in the face
of a grandchild? On a stuccoed wall hangs
a moss-eaten picture of him away at war,
cast into the campagna glare of Basso Piane,
an influenza home for drivers at the front.
But here's Hemingway as well!—fabulist,
lady-killer, Cuban pummeller of nurse sharks—
behind him my Granddaddy reads *Evangeline*
out loud at dusk, the very trocheed lines he
later coddled into me when I was half his age,
another of the poet-soldiers of the family,
another casting lovesick tired eyes at strangers,
a one to disallow the certainty of God or loneliness
and help stray silent black sheep from the fold.

Photographer Unknown, Tulsa Historical Society

WILLIAMS DREAMLAND THEATER

I passed through Harlem Sundays only as a child; the trip in
from my whitebread world was heaven and it was horror:
eggs sold singly in the snow on Lenox Avenue so cheered
my heart I thought to be a surgeon. But the gaunt
cheeks of Langston's laugh blew straight into
my skinny, limp-lunged cage of bones. Foster brother
Roger lived off Adam Clayton Powell Jr. Boulevard,
where all the empty tenements bore world's-end
hand-written scripts across the white-tin casements.
We were ten different-colored kids, poking at sore spots,
joking at an ebony piano, or the giant bowls of Corn Flakes.
Mrs. Rabain sat on a satin couch and unspun stories
none of us owned up to, sweeping back to the fires
in Tulsa's Negro Wall Street, the rioting that caught folks
unaware in Williams Dreamland Theater. White ash,
cinders, where our relations meet: first on one side of the tracks
in Boley, Oklahoma, and now, here, divided by an El
and Conte Caskets, in a city sick with fear. After gossip, grits,
greens and toast those rainy afternoons, we'd sprawl
above the avenue to watch tv, as the Moms lit up the tube
with all the news from Akron, Memphis, and Thermopylae.

II

The past has been a mint
Of blood and sorrow.
That must not be
True of tomorrow.

Langston Hughes

Hans Hubbmann, courtesy of Benteler Galleries

SOWJETUNION

Close as we are, what can we suppose of the midnight sky
or a moon that looms over the fields beyond them?
Here at arm's length, the two lie crumpled in
each other's arms, in an ox-bow trench
behind the lines of Stalingrad.
Near one, a hand-wrought iron ball from
an earlier civil war, handfuls of Saltines,
letters from his father, who is somewhere
back in a cattle valley of the Ukraine.
What was their sacrifice or bravery,
to die for a bunker that housed a brewery?
One of the letters even says that beer
goes bad in a no-man's-land.
From down in the soggy bottom
of this foxhole, you feel the cold
of underearth, and see that clouds by day
and stars by night are all there is.
If this wasn't enough, we see that life
itself is naught, like the cut-off
ox-bow of a river, when the men
can't rise and return to their homes.

Ansel Adams, Library of Congress

VOLLEYBALL, MANZANAR, SIERRAS

A still life set in apple orchards on the plains of Uz,
a meadow heath just east of Mesa Verde, today
the game is lilting out beyond 21-2, girls lifting
their breasts to the sky before it's 1942, before it's
too late to turn back, before it's time to translate
every Nisei myth as a mote in the pensioned fist
of Buddha. Before smiles, fumbling gestures
in a native tongue—respect for foreign fatherland
redoubled—the strain's so much that many grandkids
won't live out their thirties in this dirty kingdom
of the proud we call Camp Topaz. This cage of bliss,
the concentration camp we're careful not to speak of
at the store, spreads past concertina wire of a gabled
Methodist church, sheer of the fabric of the final tale.
My friend's father spent three years here counting tokens
in a coin-op laundromat—the Grand Tetonic armature
is a winter landscape Ansel Adams and *Hiroshima's*
Hersey can't resist: the pleasures of dust-hut
desert music of the purpled hills, where a white-laced
volleyball socks up over word-shy players, and apogees
the earth to overlap a reeling and burgeoned moon.

Dmitri Baltermans, Citizens Exchange Council

GRIEF, KERCH

A snow-bound road, high above the world of winnowers,
fleshers, balers, cabbages and corn.
Here the panzers trampled every hayrake down
and mangled spokes of every horse-drawn
lorry for the dead. For as far as you can see,
the bodies stretch in twos and threes
across these uninhabited plateaus.
A man on crutches comes to claim his son
as clouds roll in, dark as the dirge
of crows which feed on frozen mulberries
below in a rutted gulch.
One mother courage spreads her arms
as if to embrace all hundred thousand
lying there, with a single syllable or breath.
Another bends to a puddle, prods a mirrored corpse
still quivering, shining the last whites
of his eyes up to the parting gates of heaven.
From beyond the hills and villages, from the Caucasus
and the Caspian Sea, a journalist appears
on foot quite accidentally, like you and me,
and makes of this world a camera obscura.

Wolf Strache, courtesy of Benteler Galleries

REISE IN DIE VERGANGENHEIT
for Elvira Reith

Eyes agog in a gas mask, wrapped in burlap sacks
against the cold, a pale young mother
pushes her cracked-rim pram up Kurfurstendamm
to the Kino-Theater, the only upright
structure which holds. Deep in goose down,
her child has one of a thousand dreams
of Krystallnacht, paths down to the suckling
Holstein milch cows, a future when the Wall
will be built and then torn down.
The movie marquis scallops in sheets
of falling plaster mesh, still boasting
the coming attraction, *Journey to the Past,*
a science-fiction film of pteranodons,
sipping politely from unpolluted creeks,
lost in a valley we can't go back to.
In a matter of days, smoke will claim them both,
so this is our farewell: she in her witches'
robes, legs spread wide apart for one more
birth in her skirts, mosquito-eyed, flying from
the upturned curbstones and continual rain
of mortar, to find a flower still in bloom.

Jack Delano, Air Service Command, Library of Congress

EARLY MORNING CALISTHENICS

On Daniel Field, the Civil War's a hundred years behind us.
Georgia is peaches and peanuts and twenty-eight hundred men
preparing to protect the states from Krauts. Half of them
have skin as dark as rose or oil of oleander, half sing
boot-camp runaway blues to Oliver and Armstrong.
Howsoever they manage it, in a collective voice as deep
as the cumulo-nimbus clouds are high, they chant
an ode so blathered and happy, it's made of one
solid stone of *is*—jumping-jack in perfect unison,
four, five, six; nineteen, twenty, and twenty-one:
waking is a weapon of the soldier's arms,
each breath's a syncopated act fanatic,
a shy-worn promise that fires the greener gods,
each heart fine fodder for each new fist of family,
a sore old blackened eye of domesticity or bliss,
big black boot a turncoat's winter compass,
the mind a bed for calamus and Spanish moss,
each voice a tremulous G-clef scoring the sky,
the lemon beauty of recruits near goofy and dazzling,
the shadow of each athlete an angel of the odd and obdurate;
each swell and jump is one cadet, alive and full and sexual.

Emmanuel Evzerkhin, Union of U.S.S.R. Journalists

FIGHT TO THE DEATH

Across the steppes of Kursk, Kazakhstan, the army partisans
march to the shock-shelled howitzers
or dance to the lonesome craw of moon.
One man's jaw is bandaged shut—
what he tastes is cattle grass, gunpowder-black,
the rotten stench of the blessed but dead.
The bullet puncture in his head
is cavernous, not unlike the soft cat's-paw
it was some twenty years ago,
this one now sore and blistering
lets in the scattering ashes and tumult
of the plains. Where once a soul was issued in,
only the remnants of a driving rain intrude
and dampen his will to live. Gadflies pillage
what's left of his left cheek's flesh
and the slope of his back follows the turn
of an anti-aircraft gun that pummels at the sod.
Bent double like him, this army of somnambulists
plods on towards a river and its thirst,
while above in what's left of trees, a fist
of starlings tightens, lets go, and hastens skyward.

Photographer Unknown, U.S. Defense Department

JOE LOUIS IN ITALY, 1944

In his mouth is a wad of regulation Wonder Bread,
cube steak, beans, and mess-tin ravioli.
Other sergeants around him, mostly from Tennessee,
sip Madeira out of battered metal cups
as the white men look on from separate tables,
eager to get him into the ring.
On the barracks walls behind the champ
are aerial maps of southern France,
juice-stained Belgium, the boot of Calabria
which kicks at ripped-out pin-up girls,
splayed and taped to sweaty cinderblocks.
Their long legs stretch as if to allow
each serviceman to enter once: a dark Turk
sits in a corner, slurping soup, dreaming of fatty
breasts on Hedy Lamarr, Betty Grable's breathing
under water, riding the red-haired Asian lady
of the machete. But every time Joe spits
or gulps more water, the conversation stops—
the object of desire is here and in the flesh,
everybody smiling at the truce they've reached
until one war is over and another starts.

Barrett Gallagher, courtesy of the photographer

BURIAL AT SEA

Forty knots, a bugle call—our heads bowed down in sorrow.
As for the others, medallioned, cold in body bags,
they jettison to the bottom of the Coral Sea.
We bend to the angle of their descent and weep,
weep for those of us who are going home.
A reveille for souls, and flesh for the sharks
that surface-feed the archipelagoes of Asia.
From Leyte and Mindanao, Adak and the Aleutians,
we hear an ocean's fury, sirens of a ghost ship sailing.
At dusk, to a crimson swelling in the sky
we heft our nine cocoons to the gunnels
and pitch them over, blessed by Christ
they scuttle downwards to where there is no light.
And the ship—the *USS Intrepid*—makes for
the Port of New York, having saved the world
from the threadbare threat of a burning coast.
But each atoll is destroyed, each pearl of the sea
is black and razed, its dunes collapsing at midnight.
As for us, the salt-bit seamen of Billy Budd,
we sleep above the restless graves tonight
and dream the day when the dead shall rise in laughter.

Photographer Unknown, National Archives

DESTROYED FLYING FORTRESS
(PHOTOGRAPHER UNKNOWN)

After the automatic eye clicks a frame
of the sky and pivots, we get a glimpse of death's
geography, as seen from above the firestorm
that ravages Berlin, where rivers snake
through smoke-green trees of May.
A Messerschmidt's machine gun fire clips
the wing and cowling off a Flying Fortress
just below us—the black hull sails off in silence,
down to the suicide graves of the poet Kleist,
along the riding paths of the Tegeler See—
or drops through curtained eggshell windowpanes
of Schloss Charlottenburg's gardens
where Schubert sat and played klavier.
This disembodied airship, like the tonnage
of shrapnel around it, stands frozen—
frozen like the tongue that tells it—
caught in its landscape's reeky past,
like an adder that swallows its tail forever,
or the eye of a winsome God, just as she blinks
and fevers a serpent's gaze at man and war,
just where we're left to brood and wander.

Photographer Unknown, Weimar State Archives

GOETHE'S OAK

I stood in a fog before the pile of shoes in an exhibition hall,
black bratwurst all that was left of odors out of Buchenwald.
A glass vitrine showed books on moons mesmeric, centipedes,
a bit of quantum physics, no Nils Holgersen (a boy who flew
with swans), all music unharmonic, the tone-deaf tuning fork
of Prussia. A plaque claimed inmates were socialists, fighting
the rout of Munich's beer hall men. No Jews or Leipzig dykes,
no interning of dissidents after the Iron Curtain blew, graves
on the hill where snow still blankets a historiography of crows.
A metal button in the grass. You could hear Mephisto's cough
there, what once bore Goethe to this tree—the ochre fulcrum
of the camp—in search of temporality, to cease the panic flow
of creativity which reeled one poet so far from where he was.
Verweile doch, du bist so schön, one bird's skeletal remains
the gates we pass through back to blackest ice, warm milk
of the woods of undesire. Great liars of Thuringia huddled
here that one bleak winter before the camp was freed, children
of the barbs painting faces indigo for Faßnacht, and exiting
the world beyond the Dora factory V-8 engine room, through
a door to birchlands, where only a god of nettle-fluff or cesium
could quiet the whey-crapped mouth of another dawn coming on.

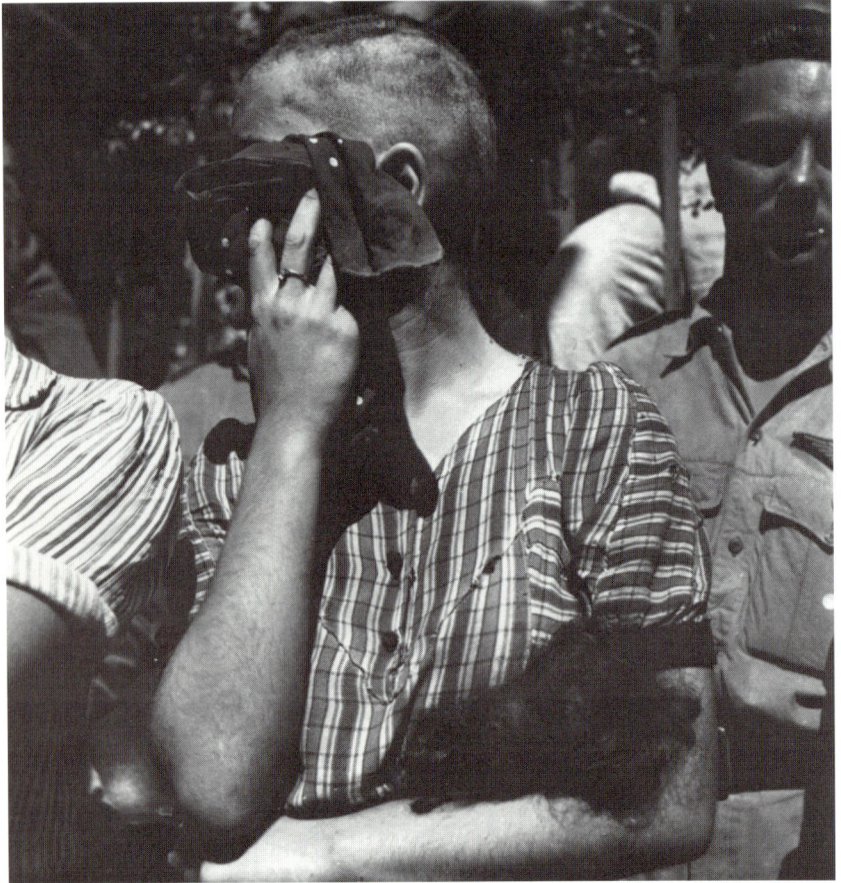

Constance Larrabee, courtesy of the photographer

COLLABORATEURS, ST. TROPEZ

Paraded up a boulevard of plane trees and umbrella pines
from the Quai Jean Jaurés, by the break-neck jetty
where a headless saint with his cock and dog
sailed in from Pisa in 66, six young mothers
and a homosexual man sweat Paul's passion
through Rue Misericorde, up the grassy knoll
to the hexagonal dungeon of the citadel.
Swastikas of ash are fingered on their foreheads
above shaved scalps and tattooed knees—
a girl made of violets holds a blue-eyed child
in her arms, can't even say, like others, she hadn't
wanted to be sleeping with the enemy.
Already the old Greek port is mined by night,
sacked by the shock troops beached at Pampelonne,
already the Saracens are returning—the naked
bathers, Colette, Cocteau, Brigitte Bardot who lives
for the green parakeets in limp-petaled rock rose,
the cork oaks and convolvulus. But Vichy's
usurpation of the role of Joan of Arc will never be
forgotten, nor will the ones who were burned at the stake
for the sake of those who stayed silent, or resisted.

Margaret Bourke-White, National Archives

INTERIOR VIEW, LEIPZIG

A clock has stopped at quarter to nine this morning.
The family is laid out, as if for three caskets,
sprawled over damasked leather furniture.
A bivouac of Americans tramps through streets,
searching out stragglers of the Viking Panzer-men.
This could be Freud's study in the Berggasse,
but for Herr Lisso, treasurer of Leipzig,
who sits with his head upon a marble desktop
as if lost in thought. Frost streaks
the open windows—they've all three
just taken a dose of cyanide, cheeks empurpled,
like co-conspirators of Oedipus or Akhnaton.
The daughter in a pressed Red Cross uniform
maintains the calm of her life, pressing between
two fingers her lover's locket and a charm.
The impeccable wife's mouth trickles blood
that spots the Turkish rug. Yellow parchments,
medieval geneologies, scattered cinders sail,
as Lisso merely folds his hands and waits.
A radiator lisps. Beyond it in a brake of trees
a mother magpie by the undulating river shrills.

Lee Miller, Lee Miller Archives

DEAD GERMAN SS PRISON GUARD

Under the blood-clogged waters and the river weeds,
in a concrete channel that surrounds the camp,
his head weighs like a stone in leafy muck,
where a dead dog grins, where pearl-shelled snails
and a gypsy's amethyst rings were thrown.
His legs in heavy, studded boots float up
to ripple the water strider's path.
Known now to no one, like Mary Shelley's monster,
he finds a final resting place near ice-bound Alps,
near to the few who might have loved him.
His yellow bloated soggy skin barely covers
the veins and arteries of his face and scalp,
where long dark hair tangles with the worms.
Late on the day of American liberation,
the fingernails on his immense right hand keep
lengthening, and his watery eyes open into
everlasting sleeplessness, his thin black lips
now part to whisper what cannot be said,
some turn of phrase to give back breath one day
to the Dachau moors, which once
were known and sung and loved for poetry.

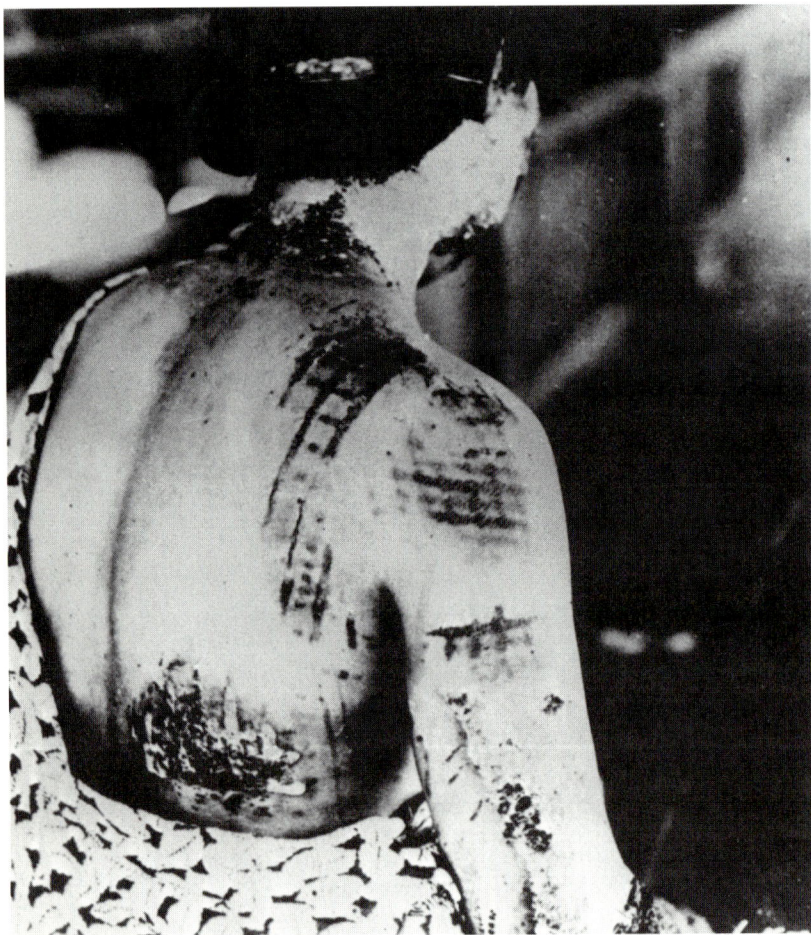

Kimura Kenichi, Library of Congress

SHADOWS

From the foothills, you can see traffic on Nagasaki Bay—
Dutch bumboats lorry crates of turnips in hock
for yams, mullet roe and breamfish, where once
a bodiless horse ran by this river in a red fog.
From the lookout at Inasa, you can almost see
shadows of mustard sedge, etched into the smouldered stone
of a cathedral—fescue blooms by an overturned tramcar
in what once was a forest of foxes and badgers
and the laughing of a maidenhair tree.
Human armbones, femora, now terrace the orchards
where smell of suppurated skin and silence reigns.
In what was left of the penitentiary, 300 yards from
the center of the blast, physicians dabbed with tweezers,
cotton, and mercurochrome upon the floral patterns
on her upper back, now indelibly hers. But Miyoko,
older now, a Madam Butterfly to the West, no longer
marvels at shadows without bodies to cast them
as she recounts this past August's Bon Matsori,
when tiny boats, filled with lanterns and sunume,
are set free in the shoals for all the departed souls
who linger offshore, jeering us, till we brim the tide.

III

Thou wert better in a grave
than to answer with thy uncovered body
this extremity of the skies.

William Shakespeare, *King Lear*

Photographer Unknown, U.S. Defense Department

THE MARCH TO CALUMNY

Throckmorton's troops are already out of it—even the segregated
jíbaro 65th Infantry plods towards Chosin Reservoir
and Lin Piao, the snow-covered Taebek Mountains,
where a bear first gave birth to humans,
boot-rot eating their feet away, houseboys and refugee girls
as sex toys in tow, to undermine bridges along the Yalu
and prepare for the bombing of Manchuria.
Here—closer to the DMZ, an iron triangle of Chinese volunteers,
below a twisted shelf-like road where the largest ginkgo
in the world glints gold—Marines lead NKPA prisoners
through terraced rice fields, half-tracks smouldering, a hole
where a hamlet was, to the dungeons of the island of Koje-Do.
Late dusk comes, fireflies, new moon, someone gestures
back to where a single stork wades in a dry creek bed,
the only trickle an ichorous bleeding of the gods.
In caves on a finger of a numbered hill, a munsin conjuress
calls up spirits from rocks and trees, the flower soldiers
of the Three Kingdoms of Korea, to celebrate Day 100
in a child's life, when the first photo is to be taken.
But there's no film in the village—no village left at all—
the chances of capturing her smile are next to nothing.

Photographer Unknown, courtesy of NACLA

SANTO DOMINGO, KILOMETRO OCHO, R.D.

Sencillamente triste, triste y torvo, triste y acre.   Pedro Mir

Off the butt of a standard-issue rifle: the rose-blue swollen eye
of a tabloid printer from Santiago—out of his clenched
and chocolate fist: grenadine, gardenias, hand-grenades
for a dictator of marshalled thoughts. The lecture on Trotsky
let out too soon: U.S. troops arrived from Camp Lejeune,
tuned to the slide of sea towards Haiti and all that sentimental
slop about whale sharks. At age eight, Rudi Acosta and I sat
back on camp cots a sea apart to wait out the invasion
of Tres Ojos. Trujillo's World's Fair paid back whatever
a caudillo owed the States—out on a barque he squat and shat
into a billiard bag. At home, the cinemas and squalor
were on fire. Liar that he was, he sang that Mir song
sweet and thunderous to little girls of sugar made
his mothers and lovers and confessors:

> *Hay un pais en el mundo*
> *colocado en el mismo trayecto del sol*
> *oriundo de la noche.*

I tried to love the wretch from where I was, but it was
thirteen years till I could see for myself what was left
of that monsoon, those headlands our families pillaged
for rum and Coke, rare bright birds, and cane to suck on.

Photographer Unknown, courtesy of Frederika Newton

AT THE NURSERY OF A LOCOMOTIVE PARTS
PLANT NEAR BEIJING

Huey Newton and the other Panthers stand around a sandbox
where six single children with little red books
and brush-and-ink sing and dance the tale
of Mao's Long March to the Yellow Sea,
of Ling Ch'ung the Leopard-Headed as he clobbers
robber-barons in their swampy, mountain lair.
Far from the rain-dust streets of Oakland,
where a cop kills a kid for trailing a patrol car
and militants in black berets sip bitter dogs
and rap to Fanshen, Ho Chi Minh, Bakunin,
here, as the old Confucian proverb goes,
all men are brothers, at least for an afternoon.
Just this side of the treeless hills, a sinewy mimosa
stiffens in the breeze and bursts its feathery
aromatic seed upon a yard of oversized propellers.
From where we are now, it's easy to see how
the image of the vanguard of the revolution—
to be bad-assed, beautiful, and black in America—
has been quashed, though for a moment
in this other world, it seems that Huey is happy
and the children are thankful for the visit.

Photographer Unknown, American Red Cross

HEARTBREAK HOTEL

Here I sit, dumbfounded, at the old French jail in Hanoi
with a strain of mosquito buzzing in my ear.
Here they don't peel back fingernails or burn off your balls—
but it's just six years of no sleep, no dreams.
With dysentery, I sit most of the day
on a rice pot, covered with leeches, half-detached
from my physical body. If only I could finish
this letter to you, or say what I must to be released.
I can't identify this war at all, the brutality
of the conquerors, the empty theater of the idealists—
all I know is there's a lake outside, lovely, blue,
maybe there are swans. I could sit and sip iced tea,
tease a tree shrew who nibbles at red peppers, pull
at tresses in a girl's hair, read to her from my phrasebook,
far, car, star... or simply sing. Maybe not come home.
Don't ask me to conjure the strafing and the napalm,
my racketing down to the forest floor, or the sleek
sweptback wings moving off through sonic boom.
No, now it's only this spider and me in our Shangri-La,
no diary, no condemnations, I don't even think I can write
to you and ask *Will you come? When will I be free?*

Photographer Unknown, courtesy of the author

REMEMBERING ULRIKE MEINHOF

Land flows into her eyes through the record player in her cell,
recording the scratched and pallid palates of a dirt band
doing sleep songs, electric bass dance rites of war.
Deep Purple down and islanded way off East,
long after raisin-bombers have blanketed the corn.
The record spins the last time for Ulrike Meinhof,
in solitary, in Stammheim Prison. Her cell is a wall
of books that blurs, congealing globs of water-oil
on linen, in company with suicide and sorrow, blistering
a world too small to be blown back inward. The cell
is an image of a butcher lover's strangling hand, forcing
a man to do something beneath his worth. A photo
on her wall depicts her twins, like Plath's, her solace
on a night when a banker's kneecaps are imploded.
Her picture in the paper, like a Joan of Arc, flaps
up boulevards in Schöneberg, where a painter picks one up
and takes it to his studio—this is her ultimate undoing,
an image of the state. He tacks it up, a wavering of O's,
her eyes like Plath's an image of a better day for her girls
to play and grow, her terrorist's blue eyes on fire the day
she's murdered in her cell or kills herself, which still terrifies.

Emiliano Chavez, CISPES

FIRING RANGE, ATLACATL BATTALION

Beyond the boys, tin icons of the FMLN, shot-gauge target practice
stand-ins for guerillas of the red zone, who've taken back
the province of Northern Morazón. The very day Reagan
thumbs up progress in human rights, Radio Venceremos
reports to The Times that evangelists in El Mozote
are massacred en masse, a ritual orgy feast in
thorns and maguey. The first photographer to get there
is Meiselas, who crosses the Rio Torola in bikini
underwear in the middle of the night, sun-up
to discover the remains of a thousand children
of Mother Immaculate, mother of the virgin jungle snake.
Roque Dalton's dead: the guitarristas are singing
in Managua, but here only carcass birds are leaning
on the wind. What witch is come to haunt silt terraces,
caves of an underground ocean reaching to Peru,
to Titicaca Lake, to liberators lost? She shadows
every farmer who's ever read Marx or the Sandinista
novelists, or Maria Storni out of Argentina. For now,
the U.S.-trained troops reign in Salvador, each
with a dollar of mine in his pocket, taking pistol potshots
at journalists or poets who limp away from here towards home.

Photographer Unknown, Corbis-Bettman

CEAUSESCU'S POET LAUREATE

*To commit a political act by means of your poetry is to be free to love
in a collective way.* A.P.

You, Paunescu, what love inspired your odes
to christen the Palace of the Republic, upon the bones
of what Magyars, Jews, children out of wedlock born
in criminal asylums, with crippled arms and ears, who walk,
sing, nod, thump and dance to the magic pool of carp?
Did you, too, steal flatware from the Hotel de Paris
and hunt down boars your leader took for his own kill?
You echoed every speech with *Romania, Ceausescu!,* each a daft
outpouring of bile upon the country you claimed to be from,
you rose like Speer through the ranks, the artist
the king and queen knelt down to, the supplicant of words.
Later, like Ustinov as fat Nero, fiddling as Rome burns,
cowering outside some embassy's gates, your angel-eyes
gleaming convict you on sight. If it wasn't for
some young reformed Securitate, you'd be
guttered down in that same concrete patio
as your patrons. A great snow lifts the curfew
off the night—the revolution starts to find itself
in the courage of people to speak what they will.
But what now—what poems can flood from your pen?
Which of your words can be wrought back flesh again?

Photographer Unknown, Corbis-Bettmann

BABY MILK PLANT

The night of Desert Storm I've put my daughter and love on a plane
to Amsterdam: German shepherds sniff about deserted Kennedy
for pipe bombs, toxic germs, incense-burners. At home, bodega
freezer racks are stocked with *Jolt,* a coffee soda to go with C-rats
for the GIs. In my head are only echoes of the streams
of smoke from space-shot Challenger. When I call days later,
Berlin's no longer throwing plasterstone at U.S. consulates,
but cheering General Schwartzkopf, the soldier who could cry.
The Post runs a picture of a supposed baby milk plant—
not far from the Euphrates, and Tom Brokaw clips a video
of censored enemy news: close-ups of infant formula spin off
racks in green-glass flasks, Iraqui college kids mop in European
overalls with BABY MILK PLANT stamped upon their smocks
in English, to drive the message home that this joystick video hit
we've scored was off, another Emerald City blunder, a blasted
Mozart regimen—say no harboring of sulphurous Scuds inside.
But I dreamt last night of King Khalid, of boghammer PT boats,
storm petrels fishing the ooze-flame straits of Bahrain,
and then the bluish milk in all the factories spilt, a caravan
of preemies crawling across concrete to face the downed jet
pilot lying in a pool of it, as it mixes with his blood and curdles.

Photographer Unknown, courtesy of the author

STALINGRAD, REVISTED

Winterreise, storm and snow. U. S. troops in Bosnia tonight
are few, and you, Hans Leo, lipped in your Hessian grave.
Your schizophrenic son in Moabit plays Bach guitar
and tries to maul his mother, sins of the patriarchs wash
up factory canals to a pebbled shore, where I sit
and poison mallard ducks, at Pfaueninsel, isle of peacocks,
where Hamlet's ghost is Stalingrad. A tank you commandeered
ignit and blew, shrapnelling all ten but you. Now you wander
bodiless the coal-dust mountains, for vacuum cleaner parts,
pursing Heine's poems and trying to forget you escaped
the U.S. camp. Polish-into-Deutsch in the Reich, you've
left me your Nazi-Ami poems of love for Ottawa's birchwoods,
for Arctic malamutes, for every Szczecin dream of reason
as you lap a kilo in the Diemelsee with an angel daughter
on your back, pure god of a girl's small world. You marched
East as clouds broke, gushed back bile unto earth,
trading a family's pride for sad-eyed German fervor.
But you must say, from the coalfield's cemetery tank-array,
where your soul sank fifty meters through the frozen sod,
that forgetting is not forgiving, for thirty years you've hovered
by my bed and cried, wailing the city Stalingrad, revisited.

Kevin Carter, Sygma Photo

WATER

This could be Samothrace, 1440 B.C.E. This could be Thebes,
Yoknapatawpah, Mogadishu, Mars tomorrow. The space
between the bird and girl is four and none and seven.
Exactly room for nurses, argonauts, entrepreneurs—
the perimeter of sky, of what we can do if we try,
of what we might do were we listening to the Congo
bleed blue across a waste the salt sea feeds into islets.
When the scavenger's beak is thrust into the center
of civilizing soul, mothers will run with curs and bitches,
hissing babies back through doors to afterbirth. Womb-
rot tales from idiot-savants like us with sunsick
overblown concern with craft, come car polish,
shoe creme, Pulitzer prize, and Chinese watercress—
the photographer sells this shot and goes to suck a muffler.
Where will the water come from to feed the fish
who've slipped into this ivied sepulchre of city?
So we spin the nerve-roots towards the reptile gut
that sanctions every respite speck of truth,
each solace gleaned a promise of wheatstraw grain
for those who work in charity, folksong, litany and prayer:
I sacrifice the origin of all ideals on Earth to give this girl a drink.

Margaret Morton, courtesy of the photographer

TENT CITY, HOMELESS SHELTER, HOOVERVILLES

Corlears Hook. Terns, cormorants, stotter along the fuel dock
where I sit—Pier 44 and Cherry—shanties in Greenpoint glint
first sun off their twisted tin. It's two below, I see
the breath of a man as he flicks tarred pigskin
off the quay and pitches O's and E's from the roof
of his mouth. Riots in Tompkins Square, raids at Bushville
and the Hill. One more Abyssinian church is burning.
Thursdays, after supper at the shelter, vet Toufik
consoles the sick with celery balm and keeps clicking off
Baywatch, but the others, tired from trampling
through tunnels, just want basketball and babes.
Angelo, he tries some lip-sync psalms, while the one-eyed
Slav hums Brahms. Ibrahim, the baby blond
of the group at forty-seven, is learning by heart
the Kingston backbeat lilt of Claude McKay.
I'm already in bed with *The Shining,* next to rum-
cracked silent James, merchant marine, who hiccups
out Arabic or Indonesian, a catarrh and some smelly
socks the only lullaby tonight, and Iceman wheezing
sounds like a post-partum, as we who are homeless tonight
shift in starched sheets on army cots and rock towards sleep.

Sebastião Salgado, courtesy of the photographer

KAGERA FALLS
for Philip Gourevitch

Follow the White Nile up seven cataracts, up the Nyabarongo River
to Rwanda, past diamond fields and ruins of Tutankhamen,
across lava floes towards Tanzania. Follow the lines on the brow
of a cattle herdsman leaning towards Kigali, where nettle
and bamboo are written on the sky. Up river, against the offing,
to where a star blinks out, to where your countryman will sleep.
Here bodies are bleached blue, white, now after a week of rains—
a week of uncowed terror. Boys of eight and nine will pulverize,
scared shitless, a sister into pulp when told to do so by a thug,
whose voice is insects, rinderpest, CNN—anything we've spun unto
disease or theater. A radio is danse macabre for the pale-browed
writer with a Russian name, who sits with me, a harlequin in beer
and bananas before he knows what he sees or says. A touch
on his arm is death's slight laugh. The lie spills out into a smile,
the coffee planter's cough, a Bujumbura secretary's wistful glance,
a murderer's bandana, an uncoiled river of the colonizing ear
of Bantu poetry, of nothing more than a brutal lung for lung,
when, as he says, peace is harder than looting—shares squat
with Aeschylean calm democracy, or God's hard love for Abel.
The heart of the dark beats fastest when you turn from this poem
and picture to tie your shoe, as if it had nothing to do with you.

Charles Porter, Sygma Photo

ILL-POLITICAL

Is wind across the Kansas prairie. The babyface mashes stiff potato
on his plate, in the still a tin-train clockface bangs into at four a.m.,
in lieu of a mother's kiss, left ere ten years luring on tiny cyclones
of bathwash hair in a motel pool. His lower body frets, mouth
flouts all militia talk—the only vocable in the room is *Timothy.*
His silence is mine as well. Five hours past the Oklahoma City
blast—where once I saw a moon as large as Mammon's gold—a tv
game show host chattles trailer homes rutted in a river bed, Rte 80,
a thousand miles from where he is, where I am, where AP news
can't say syllables for *a-n-a-r-c-h-i-s-t.* In orange deathvest V-neck,
his photo cameo will blur the firefighter's grimace as he, reckless,
cradles a one-year old who cries as she dies, heading for some
heavenless place that none of us will ever image. Blurred clockface
child who's mine and not mine, dust devils ebb your blond curls
to the edge inferno, where Echo Company still drills heads off
Iraqui farmers in sweaty underwear, bulldozed into a foxglove grave,
a dream of food I wake to night after night, a thousand miles
from his name. *Tim.* My age eleven years ago—my brother's heart.
No one laughs at him at a battalion's midnight dancing. The silence
calls in realm after realm of mother at the table, her whispering
and disppearances, the glop of spuds now greening on his plate.

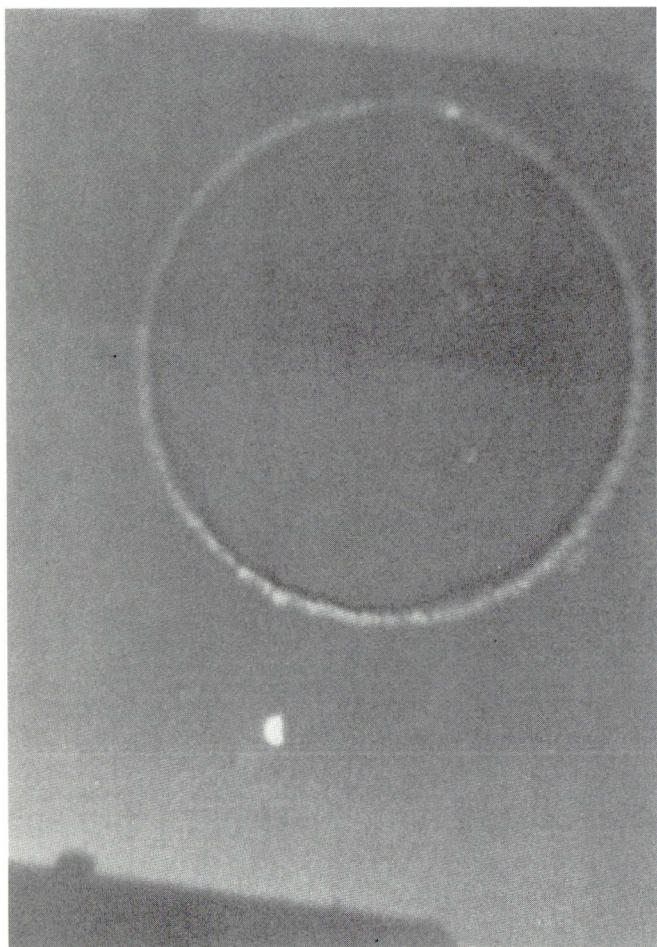

Photographer Unknown, courtesy of the author

WAR OF THE WORLDS

After my shift at the Foundling Hospital, the moon is down,
the death of a moth is nothing. I'm not alone. Ezekiel's wheel
sweeps through rocket fire, in the light of an asteroid—Eros
433—a binary pulsar that's blank and blind and homey:
I'm sick to my stomach at each city bus stop bomb in Tel Aviv.
We'd thought we'd won this one. Rabin is dead, another orphan
of Seventh Avenue is gone, and all this naming is little more
than adiabatic cooling on the planet Mars. I mean, the music
steeps each granite outcrop we call *us,* a hiss of Galapagos,
where we lose our sheen off God. Blasted heath of Lapland
or Belize is ripping a sear into what a map once was: I walk
sideways with an infant in each arm to further any written-
down, apocalyptic opening of heaven. There's fury
in ferment, there's tales to be told in images of ice or fire,
blank stares of bog men, soldiers shivering and shameless,
cold black Atlantic pillars in the dark, a starless night—
like revolutionists, dancers, or spurned desire, we smutch
our lips and gnaw the selfsame flesh that's hacked or hewn
in the rat or rabbit traps our chill-crazed mentors set for us,
mercury-bled and foundried in stone like old chintz mirrors,
shards of evil caught in the blinking retinas of every single child.

ABOUT THE AUTHOR

William Allen is a visual artist as well as a poet and teacher. He has read Pasolini's poetry at the Museum of Modern Art, and shown prints there in an exhibition called *Committed to Print*. Recently he has shown art at Michael Solway Gallery and published poems in steel and stone with Mark Patsfall Editions in Cincinnati, as well as collaborated with sculptor Barbara Westermann at Momenta Art, Williams College, and with a Children in Crisis exhibition now touring Europe to raise money for children in Bosnia. He is also working on a book of photography and prose poetry about Cuba.

His first book of poems, *The Man on the Moon*, was chosen by Philip Levine and published by New York University Press and Persea Press in 1987. After teaching poetry and literature at NYU, the Cooper Union, and School of Visual Arts in New York for many years, he lives now in Newport, R.I., where he continues to write and teach and paint.

Sevastopol: On Photographs of War can be seen as hypertext with color at: www.xenosbooks.com. Other work, including a poem cycle on Goya's Black Paintings, can be seen at: www.members.aol.com/livingrm/newport, and at: www.mpgfx.com/mpg.